Tutorial on Hardware and Software Reliability, Maintainability and Availability

Norman Schneidewind, Ph. D
Fellow of the IEEE

Standards Information Network
IEEE Press

Trademarks and Disclaimers

IEEE believes the information in this publication is accurate as of its publication date; such information is subject to change without notice. IEEE is not responsible for any inadvertent errors.

Library of Congress Cataloging-in-Publication Data

Schneidewind, Norman.
  Tutorial on hardware and software reliability, maintainability, and availability / Norman Schneidewind.
      p. cm.
  Includes bibliographical references.

  ISBN 978-0-7381-5677-4

  1. Electronic digital computers--Reliability. 2. Computer software--Reliability. 3. Systems availability.
  4. Fault-tolerant computing. I. Title.

  TK7888.3.S357 2008

  004--dc22   2008061650

IEEE
3 Park Avenue, New York, NY 10016-5997, USA

Copyright © 2008 by the Institute of Electrical and Electronics Engineers, Inc.
All rights reserved. Published March 2008.

IEEE Standards designations are trademarks of the IEEE (www.ieee.org/).

Review Policy

IEEE Press/Standards Information Network publications are not consensus documents. Information contained in this and other works has been obtained from sources believed to be reliable, and reviewed by credible members of IEEE Technical Societies, Standards Committees, and/or Working Groups, and/or relevant technical organizations. Neither the IEEE nor its authors guarantee the accuracy or completeness of any information published herein, and neither the IEEE nor its authors shall be responsible for any errors, omissions, or damages arising out of the use of this information.

Likewise, while the author and publisher believe that the information and guidance given in this work serve as an enhancement to users, all parties must rely upon their own skill and judgement when making use of it. Neither the author nor the publisher assumes any liability to anyone for any loss or damage caused by any error or omission in the work, whether such error or omission is the result of negligence or any other cause. Any and all such liability is disclaimed.

This work is published with the understanding that the IEEE and its authors are supplying information through this publication, not attempting to render engineering or other professional services. If such services are required, the assistance of an appropriate professional should be sought. The IEEE is not responsible for the statements and opinions advanced in this publication.

The information contained in IEEE Press/Standards Information Network publications is reviewed and evaluated by peer reviewers of relevant IEEE Technical Societies, Standards Committees and/or Working Groups, and/or relevant technical organizations. The authors addressed all of the reviewers' comments to the satisfaction of both the IEEE Standards Information Network and those who served as peer reviewers for this document.

The quality of the presentation of information contained in this publication reflects not only the obvious efforts of the authors, but also the work of these peer reviewers. The IEEE Press acknowledges with appreciation their dedication and contribution of time and effort on behalf of the IEEE.

To order IEEE Press Publications, call 1-800-678-IEEE.

Print: ISBN 978-0-7381-5676-7   STDSP1154

See other IEEE standards and standards-related product listings at:
http://standards.ieee.org/

About the Author

Dr. Norman F. Schneidewind is Professor Emeritus of Information Sciences in the Department of Information Sciences and the Software Engineering Group at the Naval Postgraduate School. He is now doing research and publishing in software reliability and metrics with his consulting company Computer Research.

Dr. Schneidewind is a Fellow of the IEEE, elected in 1992 for "contributions to software measurement models in reliability and metrics, and for leadership in advancing the field of software maintenance."

In 2001, he received the IEEE "Reliability Engineer of the Year" award from the IEEE Reliability Society.

In 1993 and 1999, he received awards for Outstanding Research Achievement by the Naval Postgraduate School. Dr. Schneidewind was selected for an IEEE USA Congressional Fellowship for 2005 and worked with the Committee on Homeland Security and Government Affairs, United States Senate, focusing on homeland security and cyber security.

Acknowledgement

The author offers sincere thanks to the reviewers of this publication: Lou Gallo, Dr. Sam Keene, John Musa, and Harold Williams.

Table of Contents

1. Introduction...1

2. Reliability Basics..2

   2.1 Comparing Hardware and Software 2
   2.2 Hardware Reliability...3
      2.2.1 Weibull Failure Distribution...4
      2.2.2 Multiple Component Reliability Analysis 5
      2.2.3 Parallel System 7
      2.2.4 M out of N System Model 8
      2.2.5 System Series..8
      2.2.6 Number of Components Needed to Achieve Reliability Goals...................11
   2.3 Computer System Maintenance and Availability 12
      2.3.1 Component Availability..12

3. Software Reliability Engineering Risk Analysis 14

   3.1 Criteria for Safety 16
   3.2 Prediction Error Analysis...20
   3.3 Parameter Analysis 22
   3.4 Overview of Recommended Software Reliability Models.................................22
      3.4.1 Musa-Okumoto Logarithmic Poisson Execution Time Model..................22
      3.4 2. Schneidewind Model 24

4. Summary 30

5. References..30

1. Introduction

Computer systems, whether hardware or software, are subject to failure. Precisely, what is a failure? IEEE 100, The Authoritative Dictionary of IEEE Standards Terms, has a sophisticated definition of a failure, but for reasons of simplicity, it is: the termination of the ability of an item to perform a required function [B3]. A failure may be produced in a system or product when a fault is encountered that results in the in non operation or disability of the required function and a loss of the expected service to the user. This brings us to the question of, what is a fault? A fault is a defect in the computer hardware or computer software code that can be the cause of one or more failures [B2]. A fault, if encountered, may cause a failure [B3]. A fault may also be an accidental condition that causes a functional unit to fail to perform its required function [B3].

Software-based systems have become the dominant player in the computer systems world. Since it is imperative that computer systems operate reliably, considering the criticality of software, particularly in safety critical systems, the IEEE and AIAA commissioned the development of a new standard called, the IEEE Recommended Practice on Software Reliability, IEEE P1633 [B2]. This tutorial serves as a companion document with the purpose of elaborating on key software reliability process practices in more detail than can be specified in IEEE P1633. However, since other subjects like maintainability and availability are also covered, the tutorial can be used as a stand-alone document. While the focus of the IEEE P1633 Standard is software reliability, software and hardware do not operate independent of one another, therefore, both software and hardware are addressed in this tutorial in an integrated fashion. The narrative of the tutorial is augmented with illustrative problems and solutions.

The recommended practice [B2] is a composite of models and tools and describes the "what and how" of software reliability engineering. It is important for an organization to have a disciplined process if it is to produce highly reliable software. This process uses a life cycle approach to software reliability that takes into account the risk to reliability due to software errors caused by requirements changes. Subsequently, these errors may propagate through later phases of development and maintenance [B12]. In view of the life cycle ramifications of the software reliability process, maintenance is included in this tutorial. Furthermore, because reliability and maintainability determine availability, the latter is also included.

2. Reliability Basics

To set the stage for discussing software and hardware model, the following definitions and concepts are provided:

1. Component: any hardware or software entity, such as a module, sub-system, or system.

2. t: operating time

3. $P(T \leq t)$: probability that operating time T of a component is $\leq t$ (also known as cumulative distribution function (CDF))

4. λ: failure rate (software or hardware failure rate)

5. Reliability $R(t)$: $P(T > t)$: probability of software or hardware surviving for $T > t =$ $1 - P(T \leq t)$ [B6]

6. *Hazard Function*: letting operating time t have the probability density function p (t), the *instantaneous failure rate* at time t, is defined as

$$h(t) = p(t) / R(t) \text{ [B6]},\tag{1.1}$$

where p (t) is defined as the probability that a failure will occur in the interval t, t + 1.

The hazard function is frequently described in reliability literature, but a reliability metric that is more practical for calculations with empirical data is the failure rate f (t). This is defined as the number of failures n (t) in the interval t divided by t: $f(t) = n(t) / t$. The reason the hazard function may be impractical, when dealing with empirical data, is that the probability density function p (t) may not be known.

2.1 Comparing Hardware and Software

A comparison of hardware and software attributes that pertain to reliability is shown in Table A.

You could infer that based on Table A, software reliability is difficult to predict. However, by continually refining predictions, using more failure data, and providing confidence intervals for predictions, it is practical to provide bounds on reliability [B5]. In addition, if the application does not require continuity of execution (e.g., personal computer), the software can be rejuvenated and reliability improved by restarting.

Table A: Hardware vs Software	
Hardware	**Software**
Subject to wear.	Interestingly, subject to "wear" under stressful or long-term operating conditions (e.g., buffer overflow)
Vibration, shock, and temperature affect reliability.	Does not apply.
Constant failure rate assumed in operational phase.	Variable failure rate assumed monotonically decreasing.
Accurate reliability predictions easy to make because components are infrequently change.	Accurate reliability predictions are more difficult to make because of variety and frequency of changes.
Standard, mass produced components.	Usually, one-of-a-kind components.
Reliability governed by laws of physics: minimum variability in reliability of components.	No immutable laws. Significant variability in component reliability, both at release time and over operational time.
Highly automated production process using robots.	No robots! Development and quality processes are very important in developing high reliability software, for example, CMMI and Six Sigma.
Reliability can be stated as a set of "nines".	Set of "nines" difficult to compute. Time to next failure and failure count more appropriate.

2.2 Hardware Reliability

The exponential failure distribution with constant failure rate is particularly applicable to hardware reliability because it is assumed that the failure rate remains constant after the initial burn in period and before wear out occurs. However, ore precisely, the exponential distribution is frequently used for electronic components and probabilistic modeling; however, reliability engineers widely use other classical time-to-failure distributions, such as the following: the Weibull distribution is a general purpose distribution used to model time-to-failure phenomena (its hazard rate follows a general power-law); the Lognormal distribution is used in hardware reliability to model stress-strength fatigue phenomena; Extreme-value distribution is used in reliability models for environmental phenomena [B14].

Two of the most important distributions, exponential and Weibull, are elaborated below.

Exponential Failure Distribution: $\lambda e^{-\lambda t}$ (1.2)

This distribution has a constant failure rate λ. The exponential distribution is the only failure distribution that has a constant failure rate λ and a constant hazard function h (t) in

3

the operations phase of the life cycle. This failure rate is $= 1 / \bar{t}$, where $\bar{t}$ is the mean time to failure (MTTF).

The reliability is R (t) $= e^{-\lambda t}$, (1.3)

obtained by integrating equation (1.2) from 0 to t, to obtain P (T $\leq$ t), and applying the definition of reliability R (t) $= 1 - P (T \leq t)$.

Then using equations (1.1) and (1.3), the hazard function for exponentially distributed failures is:

h (t) $= p (t) / R (t) = \lambda e^{-\lambda t} / e^{-\lambda t} = \lambda.$ (1.4)

Then applying the definition of MTTF for the exponential distribution to equation (1.3), equation (1.5) is produced:

R (t) $= e^{-(t/ \bar{t})}$ (1.5)

If we wish to solve for t for a given value of R (t), equation (1.5) is solved for t in equation (1.6)

t $= - \ln (R (t)) \bar{t}$ (1.6)

2.2.1 Weibull Failure Distribution

One of the most widely used distributions for hardware reliability is the Weibull Failure Distribution [B6]. It has the flexibility of allowing for constant, increasing, and decreasing hazard functions, as demonstrated by the following:

Hazard Function: h (t) $= \alpha\lambda(t)^{(\alpha-1)}$, (1.7)
where α is a shape parameter and λ is a scale parameter of h (t).

Using equation (1.7), we generate equations (1.8) – (1.10):

When $\alpha = 1$, h (t) is constant (exponential) $= \lambda$ (1.8)

When $\alpha = 2$, h (t) is linear $= (2 \lambda)(t)$ (increasing). (1.9)

When $\alpha = .5$, h (t) is decreasing $= .5 \lambda./ \sqrt{t}$ (1.10)

The Weibull probability density function (equation (1.11)) is flexible because it can represent software where the probability of time between failures t decreases for all values of t. On the other hand, other software has a propensity to initially get worse, as the development team struggles with implementing a myriad of requirements. Then, as the process stabilizes, reliability improves. This characteristic is represented in the Weibull by an initial increase, reaching a maximum, and then decreasing.

$$p(t) = \alpha \lambda t^{(\alpha-1)} e^{-\lambda t^\alpha}$$

(1.11)

Using equation (1.11), when $\alpha = 1$, produces the exponential distribution in equation (1.12).

$$p(t) = \lambda e^{-\lambda t}$$

(1.12)

Problem 1

Specifications

1. Hardware in a computer system should have an expected (**mean**) life $\bar{t} > 100000$ (MTTF) hours at a reliability of R (t) = .85. What is the minimum number of hours t the computer system would have to survive to meet these specifications?

2. If the hardware should have a .85 probability of surviving (i.e., reliability) for t > 50000 hours, what is the MTTF required to meet these specifications?

Solution

1. Use equation (1.5) to compute t:

t = - ln (.85) (100000) = - (-.1625) (100000) = **16, 250** hours

2. Solve equation (1.6) for $\bar{t}$:

$\bar{t} = t / [- \ln (R (t))] = 50000 / [- \ln (.85)] =$ **307,656** hours

2.2.2 Multiple Component Reliability Analysis

Due to the fact that the majority of computer systems in industry employ multiple components, the reliability analysis must be focused on predicting reliability for these systems. Hardware (and software) components can be operated in serial or parallel configurations. In hardware, the differences are more obvious because of the physical connection between components. In software, the difference is not obvious because there is no physical connection. The difference is based on how the components execute, as indicated in Figure 1. For example, in a parallel software configuration, components may be executing the same program and majority voting logic (e.g., 2 out of 3) is use to resolve faults and continue operation. In another case, the redundant components are in standby mode ready to take over should the active component fail. In the case of a serial software configuration, the components may execute serially or components may execute concurrently. For the purpose of obtaining conservative software reliability predictions, we should assume a series configuration even though the components operate in parallel.

Figure 1. Parallel and Serial Reliability Configurations

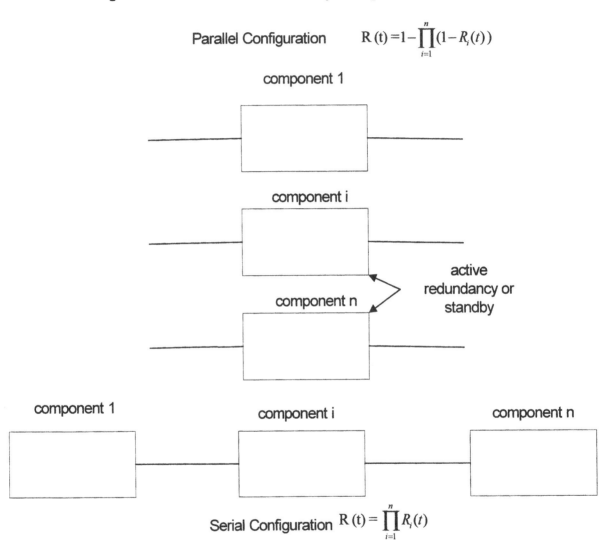

Parallel Configuration $\qquad R(t) = 1 - \prod_{i=1}^{n}(1 - R_i(t))$

component 1

component i

component n

active redundancy or standby

component 1   component i   component n

Serial Configuration $R(t) = \prod_{i=1}^{n} R_i(t)$

Parallel Hardware: Components Physically Connected in Parallel
Parallel Software: Components Execute Concurrently in Time
Serial Hardware: Components Physically Connected in Series
Serial Software: Components Execute Serially in Time

    6

2.2.3 Parallel System

As Figure 1 shows, the purpose of a parallel system is to provide a redundant configuration so that if one component fails, another component can take its place, thus increasing reliability. The reliability of a single component i, operating for a time t, is designated by R_i (t). The unreliability is then (1 - R_i (t)).

Referring to Figure 1, the reliability of *n* components operating in parallel is given by:

$$R (t) = 1 - \prod_{i=1}^{n} (1 - R_i(t)) \text{ [B8]} \tag{1.13}$$

This equation is obtained by observing that the unreliability of n components in parallel is computed by the product of the individual component unreliabilities. Then, the reliability of n components is obtained by subtracting this product from "1".

The most common parallel configuration involves using two components, so using equation (1.13) and some algebraic manipulation, the reliability of two components operating in parallel is given by:

$$R (t) = [R_1 (t) + R_2 (t)] - [R_1 (t) R_2 (t)] = 1 - [(1 - R_1 (t)) (1 - R_2 (t))] \tag{1.14}$$

If both components have the same reliability, then

$$R (t) = 2 R (t) - R^2 (t) \tag{1.15}$$

A traditional assumption in reliability is that the time between failures is exponentially distributed [B6]. This is based on the idea that there is a higher probability of small times between failures and a low probability of large times between failures. Therefore, when failures are exponentially distributed with failure rate λ, then the reliability in equation (1.13) becomes:

$$R (t) = 2 e^{-\lambda t} - e^{-2\lambda t} \tag{1.16}$$

Mean Time to Failure (MTTF) refers to the average time *to* the next failure [B8]. It is a common metric for hardware reliability because the physics of failures is well understood. However, it can be misleading because equipment will fail at specific times and not according to a mean value! MTTF is even less applicable for software because the distribution of time when software fails can be erratic. Before proceeding further, it is important to note that just because the *distribution* of failure times for both hardware and software is a better metric of reliability, does not mean that MTTF and MTBF (see below) are not used! These metrics have become so embedded in the lore of reliability that it is imperative to describe their usage.

In the case of hardware, MTTF is used when components are not repaired (i.e., replaced). In other words, with no repair, the time to next failure is *direct*, with no intervening repair time. In non-redundant software systems, the software must be repaired to continue operation, unless the fault causing the failure is trivial. Therefore, MTTF is not completely applicable for this type of software. On the other hand, for redundant software systems (e.g., fault tolerant), MTTF is applicable, with the caveat noted above.

Mean Time Between Failures (MTBF), defined as the average time *between* failures, is used when components are repaired [B8]. Thus, it is the time between failures, with an intervening repair time.

The general form for MTTF, whether hardware or software, is derived from the reliability function R (t), as follows: $\int_0^\infty R(t)dt$ [B6].

Therefore, the mean time to failure for the two component parallel arrangement, from equation (1.16), is given by

$$\bar{t} = \int_0^\infty R(t)dt = \int_0^\infty (2e^{-\lambda t} - e^{-2\lambda t})dt = \left[\frac{-2e^{-\lambda t}}{\lambda}\right]_0^\infty - \left[\frac{-e^{-2\lambda t}}{2\lambda}\right]_0^\infty = \frac{1.5}{\lambda} \qquad (1.17)$$

2.2.4 M out of N System Model

The system reliability model where redundancy and graceful degradation allows for several items to fail before the entire system fails can be modeled by the complement of the binomial distribution in equation (1.5), where R (M) is the reliability of a system of in which M = N − x components must operate reliably, x is the number of defective components, and p is the probability of defective components. For example if x = 8, N = 100, and p = .01, equation (1.5) computes to 0.999993 for the reliability of 92 components.

$$R (M) = 1 - [\frac{N!}{x! (N-x)!}p^x(1-p)^{N-x}] \qquad (1.18)$$

Also, if it is of interest to estimate the failure rate or MTBF of this system, use the fact that the mean of the binomial distribution is Np, which in the example is 1 defective component. If the MTBF of the system has been as 1000 hours, by computing the mean time between the eight failures, the mean failure rate is .001 failures per hour. Alternatively, if the mean of the number of failures per hour has been computed as .001, the MTBF would be computed as 1000 hours.

2.2.5 Series System

Often, particularly for software systems, in order to produce a conservative prediction of reliability, components are assumed to operate in series for the *purpose* of reliability prediction [B5]. This represents the weakest link in the chain concept (i.e., the system would fail if *any* component fails).

Then this conservative reliability approach of *n* components operating in series is given by:

$$R(t) = \prod_{i=1}^{n} R_i(t) \text{ [B8]}$$ (1.19)

Using equation (1.19), the reliability of two components operating in series, with equal reliabilities, is given by equation (1.7), if the failures are exponentially distributed:

$$R(t) = R^2(t) = e^{-2\lambda t}$$ (1.20)

Then, the mean time to failure for the series arrangement is given next:

$$\bar{t} = \int_0^\infty R(t)dt = \int_0^\infty e^{-2\lambda t} = \frac{-\left[e^{2\lambda t}\right]_0^\infty}{2\lambda} = \frac{1}{2\lambda}$$ (1.21)

It is often of interest to predict the improvement that can be achieved by using a parallel rather that a series configuration. Then, using equations (1.16) and (1.20), the improvement of the parallel system reliability over a series system, for two components, can be shown as:

$$RI = (2e^{-\lambda t} - e^{-2\lambda t}) - e^{-2\lambda t} = 2(e^{-\lambda t} - e^{-2\lambda t})$$ (1.22)

In addition, using equations (1.17) and (1.21), the increase in *mean time to failure* can be shown to be

$$\frac{1.5}{\lambda} - \frac{1}{2\lambda} = 1 \backslash \lambda$$ (1.23)

It is not only the improvement RI that is of interest. In addition, the rate of change of RI will reveal the rate of change of RI that will indicate how fast the improvement will occur. Then, differentiating RI (equation (1.22)) with respect to t, and setting it = 0, gives us equation (1.24):

$$\frac{d(RI)}{d(t)} = 2(-\lambda)e^{-\lambda t} - 2(-2\lambda)e^{-2\lambda t} = 0$$ (1.24)

Noting that the derivative of equation (1.22) is negative, because the first negative term decreases less rapidly that the second positive term, we know that equation (1.24) will provide a value of t that will maximize RI.

9

Then solving equation (1.24) for t, yields t^* as the value of t that maximizes RI:

$$t^* = - (1 / \lambda) (\log (.5)) \tag{1.25}$$

Problem 2

To illustrate the relationships among the several reliability configurations, the following hypothetical problem is provided: For a computer system with two components, failure rate of $\lambda = 0.001$ failures per hour, and *time to failure* listed below, plot equations (1.3), (1.16), and (1.22) on the same graph, versus t, and indicate the value of $t = t^*$ that maximizes RI, assuming an exponential distribution of time to failure t.

t (hours)
100
200
300
400
500
600
700
800
900
1000
1100
1200
1300
1400
1400
1500
1600
1700
1800
1900
2000

Solution

Figure 2 contrasts parallel reliability, serial reliability, and the improvement of parallel over serial reliability. The figure also delineates the operating time where the greatest improvement is achieved. A reliability analyst, using this plot, would understand that at $t = 683$ hours the greatest gain in reliability would occur and that at operating times either below or above this value, the gain falls off rapidly.

Tutorial on Hardware and Software Reliability, Maintainability and Availability

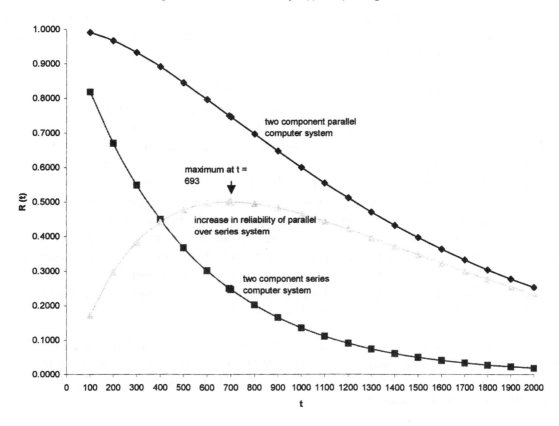

Figure 2. Problem 2: Reliability R (t) vs. Operating Time t

2.2.6 Number of Components Needed to Achieve Reliability Goals

When the reliability of a system is required to be R_n (t) in a parallel configuration, the required number *n* components, each with a reliability of R (t) =

$$R_n (t) = 1 - (1 - R (t))^n \qquad (1.26)$$

Solving equation (1.26) for *n*, yields:

$$n = \ln (1 - R_n (t)) / \ln (1 - R (t) \qquad (1.27)$$

Problem 3

How many components are needed to operate in parallel, if each component has a reliability of R (t) = .80, and it is desired to achieve a system reliability of R_n (t) = .98.

Solution

Solving equation (1.27) for *n*, yields:

n = ln (1 − R_n (t)) / ln (1 − R (t)) = ln (.02) / ln.20) = - 3.912 /-1.609 = 2.43 components = **3**

11

2.3 Computer System Maintenance and Availability

Preventive maintenance strategy: Routine inspection and service activities designed to detect potential failure conditions and make adjustments and repairs that will help prevent major operating problems [B7].

Two fundamental preventive strategies are differentiated, *time- and condition-based preventive maintenance*. In time based preventive maintenance, after a fixed period of time, a component is serviced or overhauled, independent of the wear of the component at that moment. In condition-based preventive maintenance, one inspects a condition of a component, according to some schedule. If the condition exceeds a specified critical value, preventive maintenance is performed. With regard to the timing of the inspections, there are two variants, *constant* and *condition-based inspection interval*. If one applies a constant inspection interval, an inspection is performed after a fixed period of time, analogous to time-based preventive maintenance. When deciding to perform a condition-based inspection interval, the time until the next inspection depends on the condition in the previous inspection. If the condition in the previous inspection was good, the time until the next inspection will be quite long. If the condition in the previous inspection was bad, the time until the next inspection will be quite short

Predictive maintenance strategy: Predictive maintenance is a condition-based approach to maintenance. The approach is based on predicting component condition in order to assess whether components will fail during some future period, and then taking action to avoid the consequences of the failures.

2.3.1 Component Availability

Now, in order to compute component availability, a number of quantities must be defined:

t_p: duration of component preventive maintenance

t_o: duration of component operation

t_f: duration of component failure

t_r: duration of component repair

f_p: frequency of component preventive maintenance

f_o: frequency of component operation

f_f: frequency of component failures

f_r: frequency of component repair

$\bar{t}$: mean time to component failure

With the definitions in hand, availability A, can be computed:

$$A = \frac{f_o t_o}{f_o t_o + f_p t_p + f_f t_f + f_r t_r}$$ (2.1)

Availability is also expressed by:

$$A = \bar{t} / (\bar{t} + t_r)$$ (2.2)

These quantities are portrayed graphically in Figure 3.

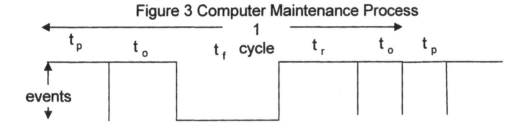

Figure 3 Computer Maintenance Process

t_p: duration of preventive maintenance

t_o: duration of operation

t_f: duration of failure

t_r: duration of repair

13

Problem 4

Given the data below for a system, compute the availability A.

Duration of operation: $t_o = 10$
Duration of preventive maintenance: $t_p = 1$
Duration of failure: $t_f = .5$
Duration of repair $t_r = 2$
Frequency of operation: $f_o = 20$
Frequency of preventive maintenance $f_p = 20$ (for every operation there is preventive maintenance)
Frequency of failure: $f_f = 4$
Frequency of repair $f_r = 4$ (for every failure there is a repair)

Then, using equation (2.1):

$$A = \frac{f_o t_o}{f_o t_o + f_p t_p + f_f t_f + f_r t_r} = \frac{(20)(10)}{(20(10) + (20)(1) + (4)(.5) + (4)(2)} = .870 \quad \text{(system availability)}$$

3. Software Reliability Engineering Risk Analysis

Software Reliability Engineering (SRE) is an established discipline that can help organizations improve the reliability of their products and processes. The IEEE/AIAA defines SRE as "the application of statistical techniques to data collected during system development and operation to specify, predict, estimate, and assess the reliability of software-based systems." The IEEE/AIAA recommended practice is a composite of models and tools and describes the "what and how" of software reliability engineering [B2]. It is important for an organization to have a disciplined process if it is to produce software, which is reliable. The process includes a life cycle approach to SRE that takes into account the risk to reliability due to requirements changes. A requirements change may induce ambiguity and uncertainty in the development process that cause errors in implementing the changes. These errors may propagate through later phases of development and maintenance. These errors may result in significant risks associated with implementing the requirements. For example, reliability risk (i.e., risk of faults and failures induced by changes in requirements) may be incurred by deficiencies in the process (e.g., lack of precision in requirements). Figure 4 shows the overall SRE closed loop holistic process.

In the figure, risk factors are metrics that indicate the degree of risk in introducing a new requirement or making a requirements change. For example, in the NASA Space Shuttle, program size and complexity, number of conflicting requirements, and memory requirements have been shown to be significantly related to reliability (i.e., increases in these risk factors are associated with decreases in reliability) [B13]. Organizations should conduct studies to determine what factors are contributing to reliability degradation. As shown in Figure 4, organizations could use feedback from operations, testing, design and programming, to determine which risk factors are associated with reliability, and revise requirements, if necessary. For example, if requirements risk assessment finds that through risk factor analysis, that defects are occurring because of excessive program size, design and programming would receive revised requirements to modularize the software.

For example, if requirements risk assessment finds that through risk factor analysis, that defects are occurring because of excessive program size, design and programming would receive revised requirements to modularize the software.

A reliability risk assessment should be based on the risk to reliability due to software defects or errors caused by requirements and requirements changes. The method to ascertain risk based on the number of requirements and the impact of changes to requirements is inexact, but nevertheless, it necessary for early requirements assessments of large scale systems.

Figure 4. Software Reliability Engineering Risk Analysis

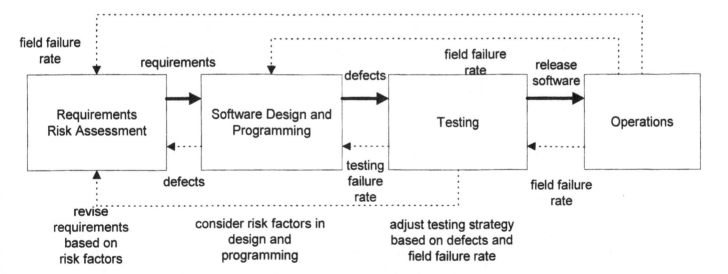

3.1 Criteria for Safety

In safety critical systems, in particular, safety criteria are used, in conjunction with risk factors, to assess whether a system is safe to operate. Two criterions are used. One is based on predicted remaining failures in relation to a threshold and the second is based on predicted time to next failure in relation to mission duration [B11]. These criteria are computed as follows:

Compute predicted *remaining failures* $r(t_t) < r_c$, where r_c is a specified remaining failures critical value, and compute predicted *time to next failure* $T_F(t_t) > t_m$, where t_m is mission duration. Once r(t$_t$) has been predicted, the risk criterion metric for *remaining failures* at total test time t_t is computed in equation (2.3):

$$\text{RCM}\, r(t_t) = \frac{r(t_t) - r_c}{r_c} = \frac{r(t_t)}{r_c} - 1 \qquad (2.3)$$

In order to illustrate the remaining failure risk criterion in relation to the predicted maximum number of failures in the software $F(\infty)$, the following parameter is needed:

$p(t)$: Fraction of remaining failures predicted at time t_t in equation (2.4):

$$p(t_t) = \frac{r(t_t)}{F(\infty)} \qquad (2.4)$$

The risk criterion metric for *time to next failure* at total test time t_t is computed in equation (2.5) based on the predicted time to next failure in equation (2.6) [B13]:

$$\text{RCM}\, T_F(t_t) = \frac{t_m - T_F(t_t)}{t_m} = 1 - \frac{T_F(t_t)}{t_m} \qquad (2.5)$$

$$\text{T}_F(t_t) = \frac{-\dfrac{1}{\beta}\log[1 - ((F(t_t) + X_{s-1}))(\dfrac{\beta}{\alpha})] + (s-1)}{for\,(F(t_t) + X_{s-1})(\dfrac{\beta}{\alpha}) < 1} \qquad (2.6)$$

Where β and α are parameters estimated from the failure data. Parameter β is the rate of change of the failure rate and α is the initial failure rate. The parameter s is the starting failure interval count that produces the most accurate reliability predictions, and X$_{s-1}$ is the observed failure count in the range of the test data from s to t$_t$. Finally, F (t$_t$) refers to the specified number of failures -- usually one -- that is used in the prediction.

In addition to the two safety criteria that have been described, safety also involves fault severity mitigation and containment. The following are some examples [B4]:

- Fault Tree Analysis

16

- Failure Mode Effects Analysis
- Requirements for what the system "shall not do" as well as what it "shall do"
- Fault insertion to see whether a system can detect and recover from the fault
- Incorporating an independent safety monitor that can, for example, check on computations to see whether they fall within the allowable range
- Firewalls to isolate critical parts of the software
- Voting schemes to validate outputs

Problem 5

Part 1: Remaining Failures Risk

Using one of the models in [B2] recommended for initial use and either the software reliability tool SMERFS or CASRE, compute equations (2.3) and (2.4) to produce Figure 5 and Figure 6 for the NASA Space Shuttle software release OI6. The failure counts for each value of test time t_t for OI6 is shown in Table 1. The data represent the failure counts for each interval, starting with the first time interval and ending with the last. Once you have inputted a text file of these counts, one at a time, the software reliability tools will compute $r(t_t)$ and $F(\infty)$ for each of the ten cases. The tools can be downloaded at http://www.slingcode.com/smerfs/ for SMERFS and at http://www.openchannelfoundation.org/projects/CASRE_3.0 for CASRE.

Figure 5. Problem 5: Predicted Remaining Failures r (t_t) and Risk Criterion Metric RCM r (t_t) vs, Test Time t_t for NASA Space Shuttle Release OI6

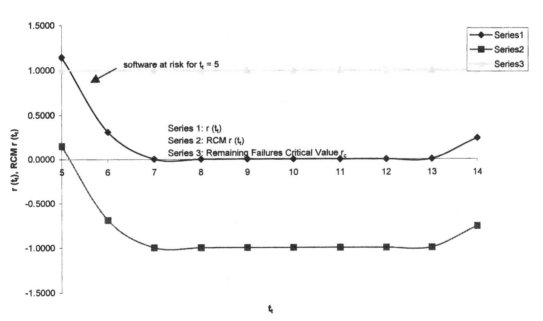

17

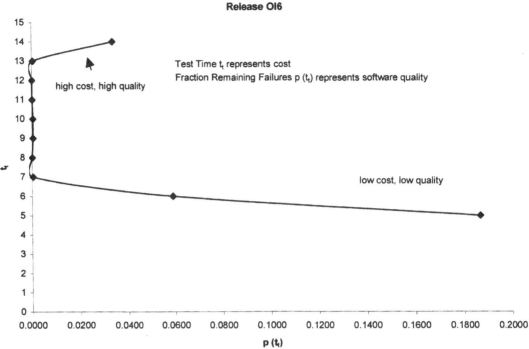

Figure 6. Problem 5: Cost of Testing t_t vs. Software Quality $p(t_t)$ for NASA Space Shuttle Release OI6

Test Time t_t represents cost
Fraction Remaining Failures $p(t_t)$ represents software quality

high cost, high quality

low cost, low quality

Table 1. Failure Counts for NASA Space Shuttle Software Release OI6

t_t	5	6	7	8	9	10	11	12	13	14
	0	0	0	0	0	0	0	0	0	0
	2	2	2	2	2	2	2	2	2	2
	1	1	1	1	1	1	1	1	1	1
	2	2	2	2	2	2	2	2	2	2
	0	0	0	0	0	0	0	0	0	0
		0	0	0	0	0	0	0	0	0
			0	0	0	0	0	0	0	0
				0	0	0	0	0	0	0
					0	0	0	0	0	0
						0	0	0	0	0
							0	0	0	0
								0	0	0
									1	1
										1

Part 2: Time to Next Failure Risk

In this part, a specific recommended model in [B2] is used [B11] in order to illustrate the use of this model's predicted time to next failure and the application of the prediction to evaluating the risk of not satisfying the mission duration requirement, as formulated in equation (2.5). Other recommended models could be used to perform the analysis.

After using one of the tools to estimate the parameters in equation (2.6), predict T_F (t_t) for one more failure and plot it and the risk criterion metric, in Figure 7, as a function of the test time t_t in Table 1.

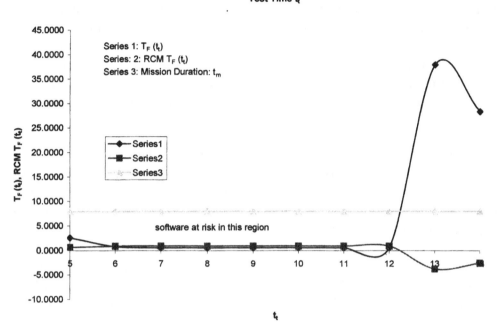

Figure 7. Problem 5: Predicted Time to Next Failure T_F (t_t) and Risk Criterion Metric RCM T_F (t_t) vs. Test Time t_t

Solution to Part 1

Figure 5 delineates the test time = 5 where the risk of exceeding the critical value of remaining failures is unacceptable. Therefore, a test time of at least 6 is required. Figure 6 shows how the software reliability analyst can do a tradeoff of the cost of testing version the quality of software produced by testing [B5]. The reason for the discontinuity is that for several values of test time, fraction remaining failures is close to zero. Since test time is usually directly related to cost, the figure indicates that a very high cost would be incurred for attempting to achieve almost fault free software. Therefore, tolerating a fraction remaining failures of about .0600 would be practical.

Solution to Part 2

Switching now to the evaluation of risk with respect to time to next failure, Figure 7 demonstrates that unless the test time is greater than 12, the time to failure will not exceed the mission duration. The engineer using such a plot would use a mission duration appropriate for the software being tested. The concept behind Figure 7 is that the software should be tested sufficiently long such that the risk criterion metric goes negative.

3.2 Prediction Error Analysis

Figures 5, 6, 7, and 8 involve predictions of remaining failures or time to next failure. Therefore, it is appropriate to document predictions errors, as provided by the SMERFS software reliability tool [B1], in Table 2. Mean square error (MSE) and Chi-Square goodness of fit are used. In addition, since test time presents a cost, we want to minimize the product of test time and MSE. As Table 2 shows, to achieve minimal (Test Time * MSE) for remaining failures, a significant amount of failure data is required that is accompanied by increasing test time (see Table 1). In contrast, time to failure predictions become less accurate with increasing test time, despite the fact that more failure data has been collected. The reason is that it becomes increasingly difficult to predict the future accurately as the future becomes more distant from the beginning of the test. This factor explains why time to next failure predictions are less accurate than remaining failure predictions.

Since the Chi-Square statistic relies on the assumption that the data can be approximated by a multinomial distribution [B6, page 774], which is not the case for the data in Table 1, we have less confidence in it than in MSE, which does not assume a particular distribution of the data. Nevertheless, it is a good idea to use more than one method when computing prediction error statistics.

A comment about the long test times in Table 2 is in order. These times are long because the Shuttle is continuously tested by contractor personnel at their desks, in the Shuttle mockup simulator, in the Shuttle Mission Simulator for training astronauts, and during flight [B5].

Lastly, the reliability analyst could compute (Test Time * MSE) incrementally, as test time is increased, to serve as a guide to stop testing.

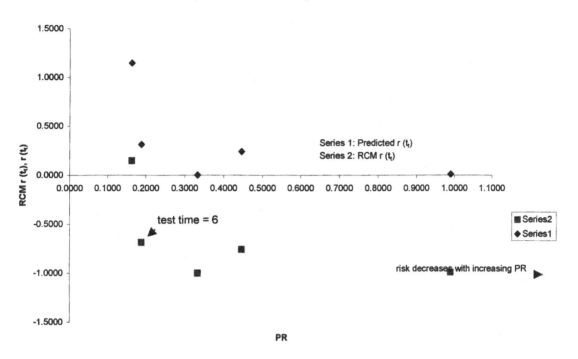

Figure 8. Problem 6: Risk Criterion Metric: RCM r (t_t) and Remaining Failures r (t_t) vs. Parameter Ratio PR (beta/alpha) for NASA Space Shuttle Software Release OI6

Test Time (30 day intervals)	Mean Square Error (MSE) for Remaining Failures	Test Time * MSE	Mean Square Error (MSE) for Time to Next Failure	Test Time * MSE	Chi-Square for Remaining Failures	Chi-Square for Time to Next Failure
			Table 2. Prediction Errors for Space Shuttle Software Release OI6			
5	.152.	.7600	**.581**	**2.9050**	**2.0154**	**2.0154**
6	188	1.1280	1.369	8.2140	2.9115	5.4833
7	.113	.7910	12.26	8.5820	3.0998	7.6117
8	.091	.7280	21.64	170.08	3.1090	7.8573
9	.113	1.0170	12.26	110.34	3.0998	7.6117
10	.113	1.1130	12.26	122.60	3.0998	7.6117
11	.101	1.1110	16.62	182.82	3.1062	7.7606
12	.091	1.0920	21.64	259.68	3.1090	7.8573
13	**.046**	**.5980**	19.85	258.05	2.9650	17.689
14	.140	1.0900	1.618	22.6520	3.1074	11.002

3.3 Parameter Analysis

It is possible to assess risk after the parameters α and β have been estimated by a tool, such as SMERFS and CASRE [B3], but *before* predictions are made. An example is provided in Figure 8 where remaining failures and its risk criterion, are plotted against the parameter ratio β / α [B13]. The reason for this result is that a high value of β means that the failure rate decreases rapidly, coupled with a low value of α, leads to high reliability. High reliability, in turn means low risk of unsafe software. Furthermore, increasing values of PR are associated with increasing values of test time, thus decreasing risk. Thus, even *before* predictions are made, it is possible to know how much test time is required to yield predictions that the software is safe to deploy. In Figure 8, this time is 6 corresponding to the same result in Figure 5. A cautionary note is that the foregoing analysis is an a priori assessment of likely risk results and does not mean, necessarily, that high values of β / α will lead to low risk.

Problem 6

After obtaining estimates of β and α using one of the reliability tools, for each value of test time in Table 1, plot Figure 8 to show that risk decreases with the parameter ratio.

3.4 Overview of Recommended Software Reliability Models

In [B2] it is stated that there are "initial models" recommended for using on an application, but if these models do not satisfy the organization's need, other models that are described in the document could be used. Since this tutorial has included several practice problems, based in part on models, an overview is presented of two of the initially recommended models: Musa-Okumoto and Schneidewind. The third mode, Generalized Exponential, involves a great amount of detail that cannot be presented here. For readers interested in more detail on these models or to learn about the other models, the recommended practice can be consulted.

3.4.1 Musa-Okumoto Logarithmic Poisson Execution Time Model

Objectives

The logarithmic Poisson model is applicable when the testing is done according to an operational profile that has variations in frequency of application functions and when early fault corrections have a greater effect on the failure rate than later ones. Thus, the failure rate has a decreasing slope. The operational profile is a set of functions and their probabilities of use [B9].

Assumptions

The assumptions for this model are:

— The software is operated in a similar manner as the anticipated operational usage.

— Failures are independent of each other.

— The failure rate decreases exponentially with execution time because faults are discovered and removed from the code.

Structure

From the model assumptions we have:

$\lambda(t)$ = failure rate after t amount of execution time has been expended $\lambda_0 e^{-\theta \mu(t)}$

The parameter λ_0 is the initial failure rate parameter and θ is the failure rate decay parameter with $\theta > 0$.

Using a re-parameterization of $\beta_0 = \theta^{-1}$ and $\beta_1 = \lambda_0 \theta$, then the estimates of β_0 and β_1 are made, as shown in, according to equations (2.7) and (2.8), respectively:

$$\hat{\beta}_0 = \frac{n}{\ln(1 + \hat{\beta}_1) t_n} \tag{2.7}$$

$$\frac{1}{\hat{\beta}_1} \sum_{i=1}^{n} \frac{1}{1 + \hat{\beta}_1 t_i} = \frac{n t_n}{(1 + \hat{\beta}_1 t_i) \ln(1 + \hat{\beta}_1 t_i)} \tag{2.8}$$

Here, t_n is the cumulative CPU time from the start of the program to the current time. During this period, n failures have been observed. Once estimates are made for β_0 and β_1, the estimates for θ and λ_0 are made in equations (2.9) and (2.10):

$$\hat{\theta} = \frac{1}{n} \ln\left(1 + \hat{\beta}_1 t_n\right) \tag{2.9}$$

$$\hat{\lambda}_0 = \hat{\beta}_0 \hat{\beta}_1 \tag{2.10}$$

Limitation

— The failure rate may rise as modifications are made to the software violating the assumption of decreasing failure rate.

Data Requirements

The required data is either:

— The time between failures, represented by X_i's.

The time of the failure n^{th} occurrences, given by $t_n = \sum_{i=1}^{n} X_i$

Applications

The major applications are described below. These are separate but related applications that, in total, comprise an integrated reliability program.
Prediction: Predicting future failure times and fault corrections

Control: Comparing prediction results with pre-defined goals and flagging software that fails to meet goals.

Assessment: Determining what action to take for software that fails to meet goals (e.g., intensify inspection, intensify testing, redesign software, and revise process). The formulation of test strategies is also a part of assessment. It involves the determination of priority, duration and completion date of testing, and allocation of personnel, and computer resources to testing.

Reliability Predictions

In [B8] it is shown that from the assumptions above and the fact that the derivative of the mean value function of failure count is the failure rate function, equation (2.11) is obtained:

$$\hat{\mu}(\tau) = \text{mean number of failures experienced by time } \tau \text{ is expended} = \frac{1}{\theta}\ln\left(\hat{\lambda}_0\hat{\theta}\tau + 1\right) \quad (2.11)$$

Implementation and Application Status

The model has been implemented by the Naval Surface Warfare Center, Dahlgren, VA as part of SMERFS and in CASRE.

3.4.2 Schneidewind Model [B11]

Objectives

The objectives of this model are to predict following software reliability metrics:

— $F(t_1,t_2)$ Predicted failure count in the range $[t_1,t_2]$

— $F(\infty)$ Predicted failure count in the range [1,∞] ; maximum failures over the life of the software

— $F(t)$ Predicted failure count in the range $[1,t]$

— $p(t)$ Fraction of remaining failures predicted at time t

— $Q(t)$ Operational quality predicted at time t; the complement of $p(t)$; the degree to which software is free of remaining faults (failures)

— $r(t_t)$ Remaining failures predicted at test time t_t

— t_t Test time predicted for given $r(t_t)$

— $T_F(t_t)$ Time to next failure predicted at test time t_t

Parameters Used in the Predictions

— α Initial failure rate

— β Rate of change of failure rate

— r_c Critical value of remaining failures used in computing the Risk Criterion Metric for remaining failures: (RCM) $r(t_t)$

— t_m Mission duration (end time-start time) used in computing the Risk Criterion Metric for time to next failure: RCM $T_F(t_t)$

The philosophy of this model is that as testing proceeds with time, the failure detection process changes. Furthermore, recent failure counts are usually of more use than earlier counts in predicting the future. Three approaches can be employed in utilizing the failure count data (i.e., number of failures detected per unit of time). Suppose there are t intervals of testing and f_i failures were detected in the ith interval, one of the following is done:

— Use all of the failures for the t intervals

— Ignore the failure counts completely from the first $s-1$ time intervals ($1 \le s \le t$) and only use the data from intervals s through t.

— Use the cumulative failure count from intervals 1 through $s-1$: $F_{s-1} = \sum_{i=1}^{s-1} f_i$

The first approach should be used when it is determined that the failure counts from all of the intervals are useful in predicting future counts. This would be the case with new software where little is known about its failure count distribution. The second approach should be used when it is determined that a significant change in the failure detection process has occurred and thus only the last $t-s+1$ intervals are useful in future failure forecasts. The last approach is an intermediate one between the other two. Here, the combined failure counts from the first $s-1$ intervals and the individual counts from the remaining intervals are representative of the failure and detection behavior for future predictions. This approach is used when the first $s-1$ interval failure counts are not as significant as in the first approach, but are sufficiently important not tp be discarded, as in the second approach.

Assumptions

— The number of failures detected in one interval is independent of the failure count in another. Note: in practice, this assumption has not proved to be a factor in obtaining prediction accuracy.

— Only new failures are counted because it is reasonable to assume that the faults that caused old failures have been removed.

— The fault correction rate is proportional to the number of faults to be corrected.

— The software is tested in a manner similar to the anticipated operational usage.

— The mean number of detected failures decreases from one interval to the next.

— The rate of failure detection is proportional to the number of failures within the program at the time of test. The failure detection process is assumed to be a non-homogeneous Poisson process with an exponentially decreasing failure detection rate [B13]. The rate is of the form $f(t) = \alpha e^{-\beta(t-s+1)}$ for the tth interval where $\alpha > 0$ and $\beta > 0$ are the parameters of the model.

Structure

The method of maximum likelihood (MLE) is used to estimate parameters. This method is based on the concept of maximizing the probability that the true values of the parameters are observed in the failure data [B9]. Two parameters are used in the model that were previously defined: α and β. In these estimates, t is the last observed failure count interval; s is the starting interval for using observed failure data in parameter estimation; X_k is the number of observed failures in interval k; X_{s-1} is the number of failures observed from 1 through s-1 intervals; $X_{s,t}$ is the number of observed failures from interval s through t; and $X_t = X_{s-1} + X_{s,t}$. The likelihood function (based on MLE) is then developed as:

$$\log L = X_t \left[\log X_t - 1 - \log\left(1 - e^{-\beta t}\right) \right]$$
$$+ X_{s-1} \left[\log\left(1 - e^{-\beta(s-1)}\right) \right] \quad (2.12)$$
$$+ X_{s,t} \left[\log\left(1 - e^{-\beta}\right) \right] - \beta \sum_{k=0}^{t-s} (s+k-1) X_{s+k}$$

Equation (2.12) is used to derive the equations for estimating α and β for each of the three approaches described earlier. The parameter estimates can be obtained by using the SMERFS or CASRE tools.

Approach 1

Use all of the failure counts from interval 1 through t (i.e., $s=1$). Equations (2.13) and (2.14) are used to estimate β and α, respectively.

$$\frac{1}{e^{\beta}-1}-\frac{t}{e^{\beta t}-1}=\sum_{k=0}^{t-1}k\frac{X_{k+1}}{X_{t}} \tag{2.13}$$

$$\alpha=\frac{\beta X_{t}}{1-e^{-\beta t}} \tag{2.14}$$

Approach 2

Use failure counts only in intervals s through t (i.e., $1\le s\le t$). Equations (2.15) and (2.16) are used to estimate β and α, respectively. (Note that approach 2 is equivalent to approach 1 for $s=1$.)

$$\frac{1}{e^{\beta}-1}-\frac{t-s+1}{e^{\beta(t-s+1)}-1}=\sum_{k=0}^{t-s}k\frac{X_{k+s}}{X_{s,t}} \tag{2.15}$$

$$\alpha=\frac{\beta X_{s,t}}{1-e^{-\beta(t-s+1)}} \tag{2.16}$$

Approach 3

Use cumulative failure counts in intervals 1 through $s-1$ and individual failure counts in intervals s through t (i.e., $2\le s\le t$). This approach is intermediate to approach 1 which uses all of the data and approach 2 that discards "old" data. Equations (2.17) and (2.18) are used to estimate β and α, respectively. (Note that approach 3 is equivalent to approach 1 for $s=2$.)

$$\frac{(s-1)X_{s-1}}{e^{\beta(s-1)}-1}+\frac{X_{s,t}}{e^{\beta}-1}-\frac{tX_{t}}{e^{\beta m}-1}=\sum_{k=0}^{t-s}(s+k-1)X_{s+k} \tag{2.17}$$

$$\alpha = \frac{\beta X_t}{1 - e^{-\beta t}}$$

(2.18)

Limitations

— Model does not account for the possibility that failures in different intervals may be related

— Model does not account for repetition of failures

— Model does not account for the possibility that failures can increase over time as the result of software modifications

These limitations should be ameliorated by configuring the software into versions that, starting with the second version, the next version represents the previous version plus modifications introduced by the next version. Each version represents a different module for reliability prediction purposes. The model is used to predict reliability for each module. Then, the software system reliability is predicted by considering the N modules to be connected in series (i.e., worst case situation), and computing the MTTF for N modules in series [B5].

Data Requirements

The only data requirements are the number of failures, $f_i, i = 1, \cdots, t$, per testing interval.

A reliability database should be created for several reasons: input data sets will be rerun, if necessary, to produce multiple predictions rather than relying on a single prediction; reliability predictions and assessments could be made for various projects; and predicted reliability could be compared with actual reliability for these projects. This database will allow the model user to perform several useful analyses: to see how well the model is performing; to compare reliability across projects to see whether there are development factors that contribute to reliability; and to see whether reliability is improving over time for a given project or across projects.

Applications

The major model applications are described below. These are separate but related uses of the model that, in total, comprise an integrated reliability program.

— Prediction: Predicting future reliability metrics such as remaining failures and time to next failure.

— Control: Comparing prediction results with pre-defined reliability goals and flagging software that fails to meet those goals.

— Assessment: Determining what action to take for software that fails to meet goals (e.g., intensify inspection, intensify testing, redesign software, and revise process). The formulation of test strategies is also part of assessment. Test strategy formulation involves the determination of: priority, duration and completion date of testing, allocation of personnel, and allocation of computer resources to testing.

— Risk Analysis: Compute risk criterion metrics for remaining failures and time to next failure.

Predict *test time* required to achieve a specified *number of remaining failures* at t_t, $r(t_t)$ in equation (2.19):

$$t_t = [\log[\alpha/(\beta[r(t_t)])]]/\beta \qquad (2.19)$$

Implementation and Application Status

The model has been implemented in FORTRAN and C++ by the Naval Surface Warfare Center, Dahlgren, Virginia as part of the Statistical Modeling and Estimation of Reliability Functions for Software (SMERFS). In addition, it has been implemented in CASRE. It can be run on an IBM PCs under all Windows operating systems.
Known applications of this model are:

— IBM, Houston, Texas: Reliability prediction and assessment of the on-board NASA Space Shuttle software

— Naval Surface Warfare Center, Dahlgren, Virginia: Research in reliability prediction and analysis of the TRIDENT I and II Fire Control Software

— Marine Corps Tactical Systems Support Activity, Camp Pendleton, California: Development of distributed system reliability models

— NASA JPL, Pasadena, California: Experiments with multi-model software reliability approach

— NASA Goddard Space Flight Center, Greenbelt, Maryland: Development of fault correction prediction models

— NASA Goddard Space Flight Center

— Hughes Aircraft Co., Fullerton, California: Integrated, multi-model approach to reliability prediction

4. Summary

The purpose of this tutorial has been two fold: 1) serve as a companion to the IEEE/AIAA Recommended Practice on Software Reliability (scheduled for publication in 2008) and 2) assist the engineer in understanding and applying the principles of hardware and software reliability, and the related subjects of maintainability and availability. Due to the prevalence of software-based systems, the focus has been on learning how to produce high reliability software. However, since hardware faults and failures can cause the highest quality software to fail to meet user expectations, considerable coverage of hardware reliability was provided. Practice problems with solutions were included to provide the reader with real-world applications of the principles that were discussed.

5. References

[B1] Farr, W. H. and Smith, O. D., *Statistical Modeling and Estimation of Reliability Functions for Software (SMERFS) Users Guide*, NAVSWC TR-84-373, Revision 2, Naval Surface Warfare Center, Dahlgren, Virginia.

[B2] IEEE/AIAA P1633™/Draft 14, Recommended Practice on Software Reliability. 2007.

[B3] IEEE 100, The Authorative Dictionary of IEEE Standard Terms, Seventh Edition.

[B4] Keene, Samuel and Watt, Gavin, "Developing Trustworthy Software for Safety Critical Systems," Reliability Review, Vol 22, number 4, pp. 14-22, December 2002.

[B5] Ted Keller and Norman F. Schneidewind, "A Successful Application of Software Reliability Engineering for the NASA Space Shuttle," Software Reliability Engineering Case Studies, International Symposium on Software Reliability Engineering, November 3, Albuquerque, New Mexico, November 4, 1997, pp. 71-82.

[B6] Handbook of Software Reliability Engineering, Edited by Michael R. Lyu, Published by IEEE Computer Society Press and McGraw-Hill Book Company, 1996.

[B7] Joseph G. Monks, Operations Management, Second Edition, McGraw-Hill, 1996.

[B8] John D. Musa, Anthony Iannino, and Kazuhira Okumoto, *Software Reliability: Measurement, Prediction, Application*, McGraw-Hill, 1987.

[B9] John D. Musa, Software Reliability Engineering: More Reliable Software, Faster and Cheaper, 2nd Edition, Authorhouse, 2004.

[B10] Schneidewind, N. F. and Keller, T. M., "Applying Reliability Models to the Space Shuttle," *IEEE Software*, July 1992, pp. 28-33.

30

[B11] Norman F. Schneidewind, "Reliability Modeling for Safety Critical Software," IEEE Transactions on Reliability, Vol. 46, No.1, March 1997, pp.88-98.

[B12] Schneidewind, Norman F., "Reliability and Maintainability of Requirements Changes," Proceedings of the International Conference on Software Maintenance, Florence, Italy, 7-9 November 2001,pp 127-136.

[B13] Norman F. Schneidewind, "Risk-Driven Software Testing And Reliability," International Journal of Reliability, Quality and Safety Engineering, Vol.14, No. 2 (2007) 99-132, World Scientific Publishing Company.

[B14] Chapter 3, "Reliability Verification, Testing, and Analysis in Engineering Design," by Gary S. Wasserman, Ph.D.   ISBN: 0-8247-0475-4. Marcell Dekker.

Lightning Source UK Ltd.
Milton Keynes UK
UKOW06f0957041213

222298UK00006B/122/P